AMAZING ANIMAL SELF-DEFENSE

Bloody Eyes
Gross Horned Lizards

by Rex Ruby

Minneapolis, Minnesota

Credits: Cover and title page, © Renphoto/iStock and © John Cancalosi/Minden Pictures; Design elements throughout, © Renphoto/iStock, © hidesy/iStock and © LoveTheWind/iStock; 4, © Mendez, Raymond/Animals Animals; 4–5, © Boyrcr420/Getty Images; 6, © TamaraLSanchez/Shutterstock; 7, © JeffGoulden/iStock; 8–9, © Mendez, Raymond/Animals Animals; 10–11, © jacobguide/iStock; 12, © GoodFocused/Shutterstock; 12–13, © Danita Delimont/Shutterstock; 14, © sangidan idan/iStock; 15, © ebettini/iStock; 16–17, © milehightraveler/iStock; 18–19, © John Cancalosi/Minden Pictures; 20–21, © Pancaketom/Dreamstime; and 22, © Dr Morley Read/Getty Images.

Bearport Publishing Company Product Development Team
President: Jen Jenson; Director of Product Development: Spencer Brinker; Senior Editor: Allison Juda; Editor: Charly Haley; Associate Editor: Naomi Reich; Senior Designer: Colin O'Dea; Associate Designer: Elena Klinkner; Associate Designer: Kayla Eggert; Product Development Assistant: Anita Stasson

Library of Congress Cataloging-in-Publication Data

Names: Ruby, Rex, author.
Title: Bloody eyes : gross horned lizards / by Rex Ruby.
Description: Minneapolis, Minnesota : Bearport Publishing Company, [2023] | Series: Amazing animal self-defense | Includes bibliographical references and index.
Identifiers: LCCN 2022029682 (print) | LCCN 2022029683 (ebook) | ISBN 9798885093859 (hardcover) | ISBN 9798885095075 (paperback) | ISBN 9798885096225 (ebook)
Subjects: LCSH: Horned toads--Defenses--Juvenile literature. | Animal defenses--Juvenile literature.
Classification: LCC QL666.L267 R83 2023 (print) | LCC QL666.L267 (ebook) | DDC 597.95/4--dc23/eng/20220721
LC record available at https://lccn.loc.gov/2022029682
LC ebook record available at https://lccn.loc.gov/2022029683

Copyright © 2023 Bearport Publishing Company. All rights reserved. No part of this publication may be reproduced in whole or in part, stored in any retrieval system, or transmitted in any form or by any means, electronic, mechanical, photocopying, recording, or otherwise, without written permission from the publisher.

For more information, write to Bearport Publishing, 5357 Penn Avenue South, Minneapolis, MN 55419.

CONTENTS

Surprise! 4
Unlucky Dogs 6
Good Shot 8
Lots of Tricks 10
A Deadly Snack 12
Ant Eaters 14
Hide and Seek 16
Underground 18
Tiny but Tough 20

Another Gross Defense 22
Glossary 23
Index........................... 24
Read More 24
Learn More Online 24
About the Author 24

SURPRISE!

A horned lizard sees a hungry coyote headed its way. The lizard shuts its eyes tight and . . . *squirt!* Blood shoots from the corner of the lizard's eyes and straight into the coyote's mouth. The shocked coyote yelps and turns away. Shooting blood is a gross way to fight off **predators**, but it works.

Horned lizards can spray blood several times in a short period if they need to escape danger.

Unlucky Dogs

Horned lizards don't spray blood at just any animal. They mostly save this trick for **canine** enemies, such as coyotes, foxes, wolves, and dogs. The blood doesn't hurt these animals—it just tastes awful to them. But while it's disgusting to canines, the blood doesn't bother other animals at all.

After being sprayed, canines may shake their heads or rub their faces in the grass.

GOOD SHOT

The lizard builds blood up in its head for times when it feels threatened. When it wants to send this blood flying, the lizard squeezes a muscle near its eye. It can aim the blood forward or backward to hit predators up to 4 feet (1.2 m) away.

There are more than a dozen **species** of horned lizards. Only some shoot blood.

LOTS OF TRICKS

Shooting blood isn't the horned lizard's only defense. Sometimes, it gulps air into its body and blows up like a balloon! This makes it look too big for a hungry animal to swallow. A lizard can also stand up on its back legs, open its mouth, and hiss like a snake. This scares some enemies away.

Horned lizards can also flatten themselves like pancakes to hide their shadows from birds flying above.

A Deadly Snack

Snakes, roadrunners, and hawks all hunt horned lizards. But the animal's hard scales and prickly spines make it hard to eat. The spiky **reptile** can get stuck in a hungry snake's throat. Then, the lizard's horns poke through the snake's skin, killing it.

Roadrunners are fast. They can catch slow horned lizards.

ANT EATERS

One of the horned lizard's enemies is also its favorite food. Ants! A hungry lizard can eat hundreds of ants a day. *Yum!* With a flick of its tongue, the lizard catches an ant and swallows it whole. However, if enough ants attack a lizard at the same time, the ants can sting it to death.

Horned lizards look like toads when they eat ants, giving them the nickname horny toads.

Hide and Seek

When they aren't snacking, horned lizards spend a lot of their time blending in. Their color and texture matches the rocks and sand of their desert **habitat**. Their **camouflage** can even make them hard for scientists to spot. Sometimes, people put **trackers** on the lizards to keep tabs on them.

Some species of horned lizards live in **prairies** and forests. They blend in there, too.

UNDERGROUND

Sometimes, horned lizards hide underground in **burrows** dug into the soil. This is where they warm up at night and cool down during the day. In fact, the reptiles spend a lot of time underground. A mother lizard also lays eggs in her burrow. Then, she leaves and doesn't come back.

One kind of horned lizards doesn't lay eggs. These lizard mothers give birth to live babies.

Tiny But Tough

Baby horned lizards are on their own from the moment they are born. Luckily, the tiny lizards can take care of themselves right away. At first, they eat mostly ants. As the lizards grow, they start to eat beetles, spiders, and other bugs. Soon, they will be blood-squirting adults.

ANOTHER GROSS DEFENSE

Velvet Worm

Horned lizards aren't the only animals that squirt gross stuff. Velvet worms spit a gluey slime at their enemies. The worms also use their slime to catch a meal of spiders, crickets, or termites. The slime hardens around the **prey**, and then the worms eat it—slime and all!

Velvet worm

GLOSSARY

burrows holes in the ground that animals use as homes

camouflage a coloring of the fur or skin that helps an animal blend into its surroundings

canine an animal that is part of the dog family

habitat a place in nature where a plant or animal normally lives

prairies areas with lots of grass and few trees

predators animals that hunt other animals for food

prey an animal that is hunted by another animal for food

reptile a cold-blooded animal, such as a lizard, snake, turtle, or crocodile, that uses lungs to breathe and usually has dry, scaly skin

species groups that animals are divided into, according to similar characteristics

trackers electronic devices that tell people where something is

Index

ants 14, 20
babies 19–21
blood 4–6, 8–10, 20
burrows 18
camouflage 16

canines 6
desert 16
eggs 18–19
enemies 6, 10, 14, 22

eyes 4, 8
food 14
scales 12–13
toads 14
tongue 14

Read More

Hudd, Emily. *Texas Horned Lizards (Unique Animal Adaptations).* North Mankato, MN: Capstone Press, 2020.

Lundgren, Julie K. *Gross and Disgusting Animals (Gross and Disgusting Things).* New York: Crabtree Publishing, 2022.

Rathburn, Betsy. *Remarkable Reptiles (Amazing Animal Classes).* Minneapolis: Bellwether Media, 2023.

Learn More Online

1. Go to **www.factsurfer.com** or scan the QR code below.
2. Enter "**Bloody Eyes**" into the search box.
3. Click on the cover of this book to see a list of websites.

About the Author

Rex Ruby lives in Minnesota with his family. He would love to see a horned lizard, but he wouldn't want to taste its blood.